ISSUE 1

Zeit|Haus

Editors:
Fiction - Leonard Klossner
Poetry - Eric K. Larsh

www.zeit-haus.com

Editorial

THE ARTIST'S MOST ENDURING STRUGGLE—INDEED one which is also shared by man, but let us shift our focus on the artist—is his against time; that is, intending to manifest his immortality before his physical expiration. Regardless of the medium, the artist appoints his brush, his pen, his camera as his philosopher's stone, believing it capable of transmuting the grief, the pleasure and pain encountered in common life into his everlasting legacy.

Is the writer's struggle absurd in thought and without significance in action? Constant is the discussion of whether or not the physical medium of print will survive. It is undeniable that we are currently in flux—while objects and their mortal creators are being phased out in preference of their digital surrogate, still we honor and hold steadfast to what many believe will become obsolete given not much time: the printed word. Are we being left behind in an old world, willfully remaining in Pompeii despite the approaching ash which may soon envelop and smother us entirely? We may be literature's martyrs afterward, but will man and his history remember us and the words we wrote? Will our poetry, our literature and the words thereof be preserved in the tephra of history's narrative for the rest of time to come? And if we do end up so fortunate, will the integrity of our cause crumble like the Colosseum or find itself mutilated like the arms and head of the Winged Victory of Samothrace that graces this issue's cover?

Arthur Schopenhauer: "Time is that by virtue of which everything becomes nothingness in our hands and loses all real value." Is it in defiance of this realization that the artist endeavors to suspend time, to halt it, to partition time into static, unchanging dimensions through his art? Do we not, as writers, mean to fashion our words like marble or stone into monuments we hope will survive erosion by the current of time?

Will these monuments preserve their meaning following their erection? Plato declared that the physical world itself is a shoddy simulacrum of a perfect and unchanging original, the idyllic, or Beauty Itself. We may behold a sunset at dawn or witness the beauty of creation in the blossom of flowers or the birth of a child, but appearances fall prey to change, to decay; one can only glance upon a representation of perfection, of the eternal for a certain amount of time before its imperfections will be noticed. Art, according to Plato, can only exist to offer representations of the representation's perfect form that cannot be replicated. An artist's work is but a reproduction of a reproduction, the original reproduction already mimicking the likeness of an eternal form. We as writers have been exiled from Plato's Republic since circa 380 BC. Now, it is in this second decade of the 21st century that we face exile from our republic of letters.

Allow me to repeat Zeit | Haus's mission statement for I believe it begs an important question: *An artist's cultural contribution is a document of and a testament to the time in which they live. Whether by photograph, story or poem, the artistic process is a distillation of dead time from the precious ore of memory. The artist refines this raw material until only its most precious significance is left.* Zeit | Haus *exists to introduce these literary fragments of time into the cultural conversation.*

Is such a document worth producing, and are such testaments worthwhile? Heidegger, in *Being and Time*, states that the most fundamental concept of the work is that being, simply, is time. Time is essentially finite, finding its termination following our death. Time is thus merely the horizon spanning birth to death on which we project our lives in its individual totality of relevance.

We wish our writing will survive our bodies, and, while we are living, we, through the invention and fabrication of falsified forms, invent ourselves as existing in a very physical and real world. Artistry is our raison d'être, and, even without a self or a world to detail and explore, still we would write, though it would be without purpose or without aim—still we would write, and this insistence in the cruel face of absurdity defines us as writers, as architects and gods of our world.

This is Zeit | Haus issue number one. We exist only to join hands with those of like mind, those who endeavor despite the finity of time and the inevitable expiration of essence and experience that follows. The future—for literature, for the printed word, for Zeit | Haus—remains steadfast in its characteristic unclarity. Perhaps a fatalist gesture: our hand extended through the haze of an uncertain future searching for those lost within the same haze. For those of you who have read this far and will continue beyond this editorial into the contents of our premiere issue, we are together; together in our wondering, together in our fearing, together in our endeavoring.

To both our readers and our writers, we are with you for now, but only *time* will tell for how long.

Leonard Klossner

THE BODY OF DIVINITY

by

GRANT CURRIER

IT'S A DELICATE OPERATION, FILLING A BODY WITH gunpowder. Consistency helps avoid suspicion. It's easiest to remove the organs and pack that cavity with enough gunpowder to keep the skin from sinking, after the cavity has dried. Otherwise, the gunpowder is useless. If done correctly, the powder can then be woven through the refashioned navel so that only a gram of it rests above the skin. Remold the umbilicus deep enough and the powder will not spill. Rings will catch on the ribs so I set mine on my desk, propped against the fracture of a femur I keep there. It's always the first thing the soldiers stare at when they come into my tent. Sometimes they will interrupt a prayer—*become like the least of these*—and I will finish—*inheret the kingdom of heaven*—before tending to them. They gawk, drawn to the bone's dark contours.

I sat in my quarters, strained by the dimming candlelight after returning from Reverend Weber, who requested I receive the body of a condemned heretic. I reread the Reverend's letter and consider a response. A weary and mustachioed private dressed in dirtied Union blues had brought me the letter. Every time he entered my quarters he smelled of hardtack like he had stitched his uniform from those pulverulent squares. My quarters, furnished by a strained appropriation of deceased soldiers' belongings, lay on the outskirts of those hopeless encampments. Other than my cot, I keep a writing desk and a stand to hold my necessary instruments. All could be quickly moved on horseback.

"There is a man waiting to see you, Doctor." He ignorantly suppressed a consumptive cough. "From Horeb."

They do not move without orders, but have been subsumed into the order of a new body that waits for commands.

"Thank you, Private," I said, giving a distrait salute. I sealed the letter. Though I knew he was tired, I asked him to bring in a basin of water, and to send in the man when he returned.

"Private. You know what to do with the barrel, right?"

"Yes, sir."

Perhaps sensing the camaraderie of a shared vocation in which we both held forth objects of the grave, Weber had as much gossip as gospel inking his pen. He wrote to me in his religious locution of Samuel Blick, a "peddler of polluted wares." The rhythm of his language remained unbroken, forged with inflection. "He didn't understand his own flesh or the sickness in him. He, colluding with Gabriel MacCulloch, established an illegal distillery and was selling the liquor to soldiers passing through Horeb."

I burnt the letter and dropped it to the earth, when the private, bringing in a water basin, was followed by a swaggering man. The private panted and, keeping his head lowered, sidled past the stranger. Confusion and shame gnarled his hands, which he kept folded into demure fists to hide his brittle nails, which were striated with picking. A hostler's fecal stench bridled his sedentary movements. Glancing at all parts of my quarters with unjustifiable suspicion, saying nothing, his maladroit body could have been the base of an underlit and plundered lighthouse stubbornly guiding ships through fog only to run them aground, and which might topple into the bay. His shoulders were slumped and cleaved and sweaty, and his words broke from him like dead branches falling from their trunk.

"So, you the man make Samuel disappear?"

"I am Doctor Watson, yes."

"I done carry him cross my shoulders two miles from the church."

"Well, where is he?"

"Outten there," he said, keeping his peregrine stare.

"Yes, yes. Bring him in. Set him here."

I indicated my cot.

He shivered and the tent flapped with wind.

"Says God'll forgive me fer what I done."

"Who says that?"

His long hair was swampy canebrake. Threads of it swung at his ears as he steadied his shuddering, lips turning blue and eyes half-open.

"The Reverend."

"Take a blanket. And what sin have you committed?"

"I's the one set the finger on 'im," he said, slipping out of the tent. "Told' 'im where he'd be."

Holding the corpse by the wrists, he dragged the body into my tent, silent until he contorted the body onto my cot. He lowered the man's head down and nearly touched his forehead to the lifeless one, and I believe I heard him muttering.

Many men had spoken of their loved ones with such similar, porous mettle. Their frames alter, and their backs bend as if in gossiping postures, too ashamed or sorrowful for a church's confession. Then he grabbed the blanket from under the corpse's legs. Placed on my cot, the body's shattered, crooked fingers laid on the frame gently. Somehow, they retained the gnarled scars of a fugitive strength. There was some mystery in the body. I could see it in the way his eyes were closed, in the rings around his eyes that had a depth of humility: strength had taken his peace and given him indolence in return.

"You're Gabriel?"

He nodded. With the blanket wrapped around him, he warmed, but the drooping tatters around him appeared to be flightless wings. He quivered as a still-living moth does before being pinned to a specimen board.

Pointing him to the body's heels, I asked, "Pull the pants tight?"

He had to put the foot against his chest.

We first took off the body's clothes, setting aside what fabric might be sold. Underneath, his legs had turned black with stoning. Gabriel was little disturbed by the presence of a half-clothed, mangled corpse. After cleaning the crevices of joints and holding the head under the basin's water to drown any lingering lice, I began my examination with the back of his skull, to see what bones might be salvaged.

"You check'n t' see he dead?"

"What would indicate he could still be alive?"

"Well, he were a prophet. Heard a voice while he breathe. Tell 'im t' kill that preacher, Rev'rind Weber."

The tent's canvas succumbed to the mercuriality of torches and campfires, and all of its terpsichorean fibers turned to bronze shifting in the wind.

"He heard a voice. Many people hear voices. Did he do any miracles?"

"Nones I's aware a. Say God spoke t' him."

"God Almighty?"

"Yessir."

"But now he's dead."

"S'pose so. Shame, too. Made the damn best liquor north a Georgia."

All his movements were tentative and conducted with uncertainty.

I doubted that a body so battered was the framework of a once respected man; apostates rarely carry their scars to the grave.

"He want you t' take 'im away. Gawn help 'im out real nice."

"Who?"

"Weber."

"Why does he want me to take him away?"

"People love a martyr. Ain't no killin' people fer what they don' believe. He done and gone kilt a whole bunch. Liketa have me kilt when I gits back."

"And why would he do that?"

"We don' render 'im hisn due, he say. Take ourn ten percent what he say rightly belong t' th' church."

A sound more bray than breathe came from him.

"What you gawn do wit' 'im?"

"Give him a proper burial," I lied. "Distribute his shoes and clothes to those in need of it."

Here was a man who knew the loneliness of belief.

"Won' fit none a 'em."

"They'll use it as patches. Fixing's sufficient for our needs."

"Where you gawn bury 'im?"

"We have grounds."

"Weber have grounds too. Damn fool won' give nothin' fer 'im though."

"You don't think him a wise man?"

Ain't no wisdom in the devil. Craftiness, though. He crafty 'nough."

Humming a recited doctrine of distraction familiar to those grieving, Gabriel played with the wings of his blanket. He sat cross-legged and dropped the blades of grass he had plucked.

His belief in mourning, that faith of grief, was his and every soldier's casuistic heresy from which I had dissented.

"You want something to drink? Warm yourself?"

"Jus 'nough t' warm some," he said, turning a hand from the blanket's folds to accept the glass. "Mighty cold out there tonight."

Soon, his chin sheening with whiskey that poured from his mouth, he spoke of the visions he shared with Samuel and the one that undid him. I had to sit beside Gabriel and keep him steady. His eyes were closed and I poured my drink beside me to suggest another. There had been an accident in which Samuel's mother had fallen from a ladder while harvesting pecans. Samuel, having seen her tumble, rushed from his house, but the word of God fixed him to his porch. She stood, supposedly, and lifted her hand before falling again. He buried her the following spring, and from then on refused to give the church his tithe.

"They cast 'im out fer it. All a 'em. Said if'n he din't kilt her he were sick. That's when Weber find me. Say he kin make sure I get what's mine. Say I gotta make 'tonemint afore I git my still agin."

In his testimony was a smudge of emendation he mistook for tenet. Such allusive imposture kindled in me envy and temerarity. The calmative measure for those disturbances is an unbridled inquisitiveness regarding the misfortunes of others, and an earnest effort at conciliation.

"But you must show them," I said, filling his glass.

"Show 'em what?"

"The truth. That Samuel was who he said he was."

He twisted his face which asked *how*.

"Take the body back to them. Show it in the church. Put a torch in front of him and let people inspect him. Have them walk by. Then, Weber'll come near."

Interrupting us, the private put his head through the flap.

"As you need, sir," he said, and left.

I slapped Gabriel's knee.

"Why don't you come back tomorrow evening? Toward sunset. I'll wash and fix Samuel so you can take him back and show those doubters who he really is."

I extinguished the light and had the private bring the barrel into my tent. He coughed more; small, rippling coughs that would have barely scratched his throat or lungs, but I could hear idle disease sharpening its blade within him.

"No one saw me," he said, tremulous.

"Good."

The barrel between us, barely visible to each other.

"Come back tomorrow. You'll have the relics."

His stance stiffened: the heels of his boots came together and dug into the ground, his overjacket rubbed against his trousers and the leather straps around his shoulders stretched. Pivoting, he threw the flap open and returned to his camp.

As a clinician I journey from bivouac to cantonment and offer such men with death in their limbs a chance to assuage their fears by venerating the martyrs who had known terror. With the few collected remains of men who had valiantly faced death, I could assuage the dying's anxiety and doubt. Within the martyrs there is a tremor of eternity ossified in their marrow.

Soldiers' cannon-burned faces became holy as they gazed on these objects of hope. Here were the remains of a man like them, racked with pain, anger, confusion.

Mercy, they would whimper. Blood often drenched their limbs, and fire turned their skin into char that flaked in the wind.

Knowing these bodies of divinity requires scholarship. It was my custom to feel all parts of the corpse, to know it as a priest does his catechism. And as the catechumen must start with the lofty notion of deity and work man-ward, so I began with the cranium and concluded with the tarsi. I would search for the rosaries of carpi and, though they were not prayers, in their loose roundness I would find peace. To the ignorant soldier a corpse's femur may well have been the leg of David, or its ribs the last testament of Peter. Only in the flesh of others is mystery charismatic. The only true ailment we have here is pain, and the testimony of divinity rests in our broken bones.

Still, hope may be as responsible for consuming as many lives as minié.

I had taught myself the ways of war and man, and had no need of light, but began to disembowel the corpse. The blood, no longer warm, coated my hands thickly like spoilt milk. The body's broken ribs lay in his chest like two stone slabs, and their fractures glyphed an obloquy which only my previous exposure to him allowed me to translate.

Earlier that day, my rucksack, tied to a buffeted mattock, contained Reverend Weber's letter, hardtack, and the broken bulk of a femur and half of a jawbone. I, stepping through the broom-sedge that covered the eastern part of a Tennessean field, approached Weber's church. My crunching stride galvanized a dozen pheasants to flight, and I stood watching the striped colors of their feathers pass through the air like silent fusillades. When their flitting calmed, the hammering of rock clattered from the church like an organist composing the meter for a stony hymnal. My heart sang its meter in broken measures.

Lumbering out the church's door were four blood-spattered men, stained as after a sawbones' work, though their medicine was not one of healing. They rested on a thick, fallen tree, and passed a ceramic jeroboam between them. A single man walking with a practiced, dignified posture followed them; he combed his hair and lowered himself onto the tree beside the bloodied men.

In the wrinkles along his cheeks and forehead, one appeared fashioned by a potter who shaped his vessels with piano string. His heavy eyelids and sagging jawline, even the way he churned the air through his teeth, smeared him with the exhaustion of felonious toil.

"Who's you?"

He spoke, like he was trying to flint a fire with his tongue, and spat a long stream of tobacco through his teeth.

"Settle yourself, Bozum," the dignified man said, reaching across Bozum's chest. "My apologies."

He spoke in a drumlin way, his words rising to flat plateaux of dry inflection. Round his eyes were dark rings, and his pallid cheeks sagged. Returning to their jeroboam, the four men obeyed and relaxed with recalcitrant sighs.

"Owen Watson," I said.

"Peter Weber."

His grip was a hard, fired brick, his fingers hammered ferrules.

A thrush landing along the roof beam sang without response. It skittered, arching its head, and flew away.

"One of my congregants' sons speaks highly of you," Weber said, turning his head toward the seated men in slight reprimand. "They say you promoted his healing after Vicksburg."

Hunched and breathed as through a mud-clogged drainpipe, Bozum kept his sight focused on me.

"You have something for me?"

Weber stood with a pietistic shrug, "We do. In the church."

In his stride he guarded a partible dignity of which he appeared to claim an uneven share. He walked with his hands held against his chest, folded with a shield-bearer's grip.

His church was plain and without beauty; simple, unpainted oak pews and plastered walls. At the altar's base, surrounded by white-nicked stones, some the size of a child's head, lay a man, whose chest was a tattered and bubbling wineskin.

"What happened?" I asked, stepping past Weber. Before he answered, I heard a shivering crunch. Raising my foot I saw the pieces of a small white object that had been a tooth.

"What I had written about. What I feared."

Possessed of a voice of such firm timber that it could dull assaulting ax and saw, he paused between sentences as though to give time for my own pity to sprout.

"He couldn't shake the notion?"

"Refused to listen to reason. He had a sickness of the mind."

I approached the body. His eyelids were still open though anything resembling an eye had been pummeled back into his skull. His lips were swollen and jagged where they had cut on his teeth.

"Believed he heard voices and commands," I said, recalling Weber's concern.

Weber nodded. "What can you do for one who believes such things?" Weber coughed and turned around. "For him we did what we could."

"You didn't mention his size," I said.

"Does this pose a problem?"

His shoes' soles had uneven wear, which, notwithstanding, I could still sell; they were not so worn as to render them undesirable for a soldier who had walked through theirs.

"Not particularly. Unless there's cause for secrecy."

"Surreption is our salvation, Doctor. The weak-minded will not understand. The body is yours to do with as you please. It is a grace to us that you find such a use for this molded earth. He has become a curse to those who knew him. I only wish that a profligate's life might become of some salvific use to a wearied soul."

Studying this body, I absorbed quickly what tenets I could discern, and decided how I should carry such a burden.

"We cannot allow the rumors of Samuel's stoning to solidify.

"Despite the opprobrium we have and will heap on him, some remnant will believe in an odd rumor. They believe in Samuel's prophethood, believe that his very vindication lay with his burial; that, if exhumed, his body would be untouched by decay. We cannot have him buried anywhere, you see."

Here was a wonder of faith, a man different and abused. I had never seen a body mutilated in such manner. If any man appeared weary, it would have been this man.

"Bring him to my camp. I cannot carry him. It will raise suspicions. Hire someone. Bring him at night."

Weber grinned, said he knew the person to send.

While he strode out the church, his shoulders thievishly tight, I looked at the giant's corpse once more. His face had been knocked off center, the bones beneath the skin shifting to twist an already deformed face into the cuneiform of repellence: the eyebrows askew and collapsed; the nose nearly flattened; and his chin sticking into the air, forming a small mound under his left cheek. To calm myself I touched my ring and thought of my wife.

No man becomes a saint without decay.

Removing his organs proved more difficult than I estimated. They were large, cumbrous things; his liver as large as a newborn slick with afterbirth, and his lungs the stems of ridged boletes. The stomach slapped against itself when tossed on the ground. Before such rites of canonization I always knelt. Blood soaked my shirt and pooled in my lap. The cavity does not need to be perfectly clean, and the battered ribs would undoubtedly work in my favor. The spine knobbed the muscle as I ran my hand along the now vacant cavity. Losing some of its softness, the fibers had become tense, ligneous, and I might have been delicately studying the grain of wood as muscle. From the neck to his hips I had emptied him, piling the organs on the ground near his head where I would be safe from slipping on them. Having ample cloths which none would question bloodied, I packed the cavity with them and covered him with a shroud.

After burying the splanchnic, I slept.

Shirtless and goosefleshed in that October dawn's breeze, I stood outside drinking a coffee that steamed and warmed my face as I drank. Thinking of the few hours until Gabriel would come to retrieve the body, I rehearsed some lines I would write to Weber.

Medicine is faith in the flesh, I practiced, imagining flourished ligatures and finials.

I tossed the remaining cold coffee into the fog.

The body's packed cloth had turned pink.

Dried and aired, the abdomen now resembled the work of a blind seamstress. Individual fibers stood out in panoplies of spectrums: brown, red, peach, and black where blood had hardened.

Satisfied, I kicked open the barrel and took a handful of gunpowder from it and started packing it firmly near the corpse's hips. Once filled, I stitched the abdomen and dressed him as the soldier entered my tent.

For all my study the only infinity I see is in our bones. In flesh is sufficient mystery, and soldiers exposed to tedium will cling to wonder like a corporal a general's order, so that even in death there is a semblance of obedience to authority. Going beyond our own skin involves us in heresies.

I wrapped my bones double in cheesecloth, placed then in burlap and set them in an oaken chest. This chest I lay between me and the private.

He now smelled, much like Samuel, of the battlefield, of smoke and saltpeter and charcoal.

Whenever his lips moved I thought of pondweed. He did not speak so much as recite the rehearsed lines, his brow furrowed each time the foreseen strategem betrayed him. With a yellowed cloth he daubed the sweat from his forehead, always looking down and folding the cloth twice before putting it in his back pocket, only to draw it out some minutes later. Perhaps the barrel excited him. We sat within an arm's reach of it.

"Will they heal me, Doctor?"

"The faith they inspire will, yes."

"And if I have no faith?"

"That is what the bones are for."

The conversation continued in this way, chlonic spurts of vigor where his eyes engraved what his mouth spoke. If there was ever a man unified in his fear, he sat before me. Fear had gathered the materials for him: his elaborate mustache, curling from his lips and meeting the scruff on his chin, had the shape of a kettle but the thickness of a widow's wickerbroom. Even as he spoke it scratched and made a sweeping sound. Part of his nose had been shot off, giving him the appearance, with his long hair, of a jester wearing the mask of a falcon's clipped beak.

"Why is it you've come here? To me? Most men call for me

only when they are dying. When rumor reaches them that I hold some remnant of hope here."

I touched the chest with gingerly reverence, keeping the fingertips on the wood only for a moment. It was a practiced motion, much as, I assume, Peter Weber has practiced the articulation of his voice. In the conveyance of truth, or mercy, or hope, preparation ballasts doubt, and motions of kindness can soothe as much or more than words.

He twisted his mouth to a narrow point, and swung his head looking at the ground.

"What is it you fear, then? Death?"

"Not death."

"How not death?"

"I am a soldier. I know I will die."

"So then after death."

"No."

"What then?"

He took time on a thought I expected would be of stale originality, molding it with the manipulations of his eyes and brows, relying even on the tautness of his cheeks to give shape to his answer. No one had told me that they wanted a reminder of their death, though that was why I kept these bones so close. Few had mentioned that strict curiosity bade them call me. Having years before entrusted my education to the limbs of the dying, wounded abdomens, absent limbs, and the screams of men whose diseases were being scraped from them became the chalkboards of a terrifying and arcane doctrine. Faith is not in the body to heal or mend, but to crush. I had often watched as their fear-thickened eyes clouded like stirred myrrh, rapt in a gaze that sought with their last thew the lines of the bones for hidden incantations, when all they found there was the momentary palliation of suffering before they would slip to the hands of surgeons or gravediggers.

The private was folding his handkerchief, and raised his head so that he spoke with confidence.

"They are precious," he said. "Perhaps I wanted to see something holy."

Pastors would slaughter half their flock for such a sheep. I was content merely with sheering.

"I, too, have often beheld their splendor," I said, setting a palm on the chest.

Bringing from a pocket a key, I pushed it into the lock.

"It is a quiet wonder. It moves one. Like lightning without thunder."

I dropped to a whisper and he leaned an ear closer.

"In flashes these things reveal the darkness in us because they are light. Stare at them enough and, like the image of the sun, their light is burned into your vision."

I opened the chest and drew out the shrouded remains. Handing them to the private, the cheesecloth draped his hands like a veil. He, standing, took the bone outside behind my tent, and I listened to him pray.

Whether he witnessed something holy I cannot say. His words were like the words of all men called to battle: unoriginal and scattered. His prayers were the bones of saints: ordinary dust.

He walked with the dignified posture of one completely satisfied with their possessions, unwanting in anything else. For the first time since meeting him, I saw his shoulders become round and firm, the muscles along his forearms relaxing. Of those bones he claimed an ownership that did not belong to him.

The veneration lasted near an hour and afforded me ample time to assemble the sparking contraption. Securing with a thick needle a piece of steel just below Samuel's umbilicus, I sewed a piece of flintrock into the shroud. When torn off, the flint should spark.

Death makes all things delicate. There is a precision which comes with death that requires a tenderness of touch. Before the private would finish and Gabriel return, I laid the bones on the cloth on my desk, and sat studying them until the crevices between the teeth became distinct. It is worth studying what men will become, where they have come from.

The skull's round top fits my palm nicely, its surface the temperature of freshly-chopped wood, and the texture of vellum. Nightly, I set my hand there, reciting some prayer about becoming the least of these as I stroked the cranial side.

The least of these—the dead, apostates, children.

Samuel, Gabriel, that private, Weber—these men are not the least of the earth. Poor, perhaps, but all embroiled in a hubristic defense of their own vindication. Studying the bodies of men, I think of heretics. Studying the bones of new martyrs, I think of my wife.

If the failures of our lives might be relived, how much time would we spend on them, buffeting them until they shone with such resplendence so as to cast the rest of our existence into the umbrage of our meagerness? We would do little more than polish a nickel in a gold mine.

We the apostate relinquish what we once cherished and are afeared to adore once more.

"Finished?"

He said nothing, but returned the bones he cradled to their reliquary, rising with the mute astonishment of a convict hearing their rescission that shows not in the face but in the limbs, the lightness of delicacy and burdensomeness of awe comingled in his arms, which he used almost as crutches.

In veneration we become vindicable.

When Gabriel entered my tent, his face, in its drooped contortions, was the painted face of an old warrior taking to the plains solely for the sake of honor. He strained to keep his eyes open. With voice fiddling and hands vibrated like the hides of struck tympanies, he stood beside the covered body. He asked me what he should do. I told him he should gather everyone to the church, no matter what time, that night was better, and to make certain that Weber came. He should have set the body on the altar table with the cloth covering it, for the sake of decency. I warned him and had him repeat that he was to keep the first few pews empty. There is danger in witnessing a body of divinity, and that glory, if approached flippantly, will kill the witnesses.

"Weber will come in, and he'll demand to know what you mean, and why you've brought back the body. Though I doubt he'll ask that outright. Give him this letter and have him read it aloud to the church. After this, have him stand beside you and tear off the shroud."

"What'll happen?"

"All will know the truth. Samuel was a prophet. He'll come back to life," I said, slipping the copy of my letter into his grimaced hand.

He took the body and left, his back and legs suddenly strong as though making his way to claim a heritage for which he would have to sacrifice nothing.

Reverend, I must return this body to you, as I find neither corruption, nor decay, nor use for it.

I practice the art of healing, imperfect though it is.

You wrote me, saying, We are troglodytic creatures, scrounging on the craggy shoreline of our own shallow consciences, terrified at those echoing, ululant forests surrounding us. Dare we leave our coast?

Hearing in your letter your drumlin inflection, I could not but recall that clapping of rock against Samuel's body as I approached your church. This is your praise, Weber, the means of bringing your faithful together, and I think of what might happen if we were to sing such songs of stone, if we could get hardness into our voices and put into our bones iron like the saints who guard, in adamantine repose, the lives of the faithful.

No, you continued. We dare not move from where we've been placed. We are given to the tasks of redemption, and you have aided in the absolution of this humble town. We would do well to remember how much fidelity can come from falsity. Built more of association than truth, the body is a symbol of faith and not its vessel.

Once a physician realizes that faith, hope and love render useless all his medicine, what course remains but to concoct similar nostrums and pray their physic becomes effective?

To heal one must become diseased because of sickness there is no eradication, only subsumption.

Yes, medicine is the great extirpator, a ruthless and cunning tyrant that extends its rule as its subjects increase in their knowledge; as long as we priests of the physic have as our sacrifice the willing trust of believers in our salvation, the surgeon's table is a temple to which they will flee.

What medicine did this Samuel unknowingly leave behind!

How often I sit dripping in humid tents, contemplating such things. We will care less about our souls in those days when our stomachs are full, when our veins run thick with inebriant than in blissful days; we neglect our seats of divinity, though why is beyond our ken.

I was witness to the death of my beloved. After her childbearing death I prayed for thinness, for disease and thirst, but what I was granted instead was a hope infectious and fervent, incubated in my daughter's pules. She cooed a language of assuagement from her cradle, teaching me pentecostal tongues I had thought long extinct, languages that extirpated the guilt and horror of remembering her mother sprawled in a bed of her own blood, and a dejected physician closing the door, abjuring the sacred mantle of his duty. Now in the tents of soldiers, I see that same moribund liturgy in which my beloved had participated. Disguise fear as faith and a strange accord forms between the bodies of dying men and the bones they venerate. Both come to life.

I, who had become an unfired cannon dormant with a comminuted faith, recite prayers as much for the soldiers who gaze at my bones as for me, and the stark memories of my cherished ones. I trust in medicine because by that art I am able to know my virulent self. Let us pursue emaciation, thirst, solitude, anything that might strengthen the catafalque on which our bodies are to be displayed and judged, rather than indulge in the pittance of belief afforded by comfort.

To this end, on the outskirts of these encampments, I lay her bones before me, thumb their striations while reciting a canticle, and pray. These, the remnants of unanswered prayer, of hope, are frangible, and crumble year by year in my hands, but in candlelight they burn like gold and are veined with chronicles of yearning and love. They are living testaments of stone that live for a moment in my care before they return to the dust from which they were carved.

I write, Reverend, even now hearing an evangelic cannonade beyond my quarters. I will be needed soon, and will give again a gift I have received. Surely some new encampment lies near needing hope.

Reverend, amen! What a hope we have beheld. A gospel of flesh; bones that live!

THE DROUGHT AND FARMER JOHN

and

FISH

and

THE MOON IN THE TREE

by

JOHN GREY

THE DROUGHT AND FARMER JOHN

If only the grackles, the cowbirds, tilled my fields,
the ones that, masked, raid the last of my sorry seeds.
Yes, there's great wealth in imagining.

I'm one of many: Farmer Roy, Farmer Claude,
there's even a Farmer Amy,
My silos are empty.
My wide acres are sadly sown.
I move wheels. I hammer posts.
I'm responsible for every task bar the weather.

Earth ripened and glowed like orchards once.
Scraps of hope remain, grown parched and wrinkled.
A long dry summer seizes my farm
and gives me nothing for it.
Ah, life is such a long nightmare
interspersed with dreams.
It's an empty space
continually raided, emptied.
The dirt in my hand knows
what I'm talking about.
I am its servant but it no longer
has work for me.

Another day, wide open, crammed, from fence to fence.
with absurd rows of nothingness.
I'm a farmer—make that a prisoner of earth—
like my scarecrow, a skeleton hung with clothes,

straw hastily patched together.
And, above me, shines a solar husbandry of light and heat.
If only clouds were my crop and, just by looking up,
I plowed the firmament.

FISH

Beware, fish, scaled silver
in coppery twilight water,
who swivel dances
underneath my eyes.

There's anglers
on the opposite bank
who long to make a meal of you.

You fling yourself away.
Then reel your body
back to shallows.
Your mouth opens.
Throat gulps.
Gills flutter.
Quick tail swish,
you're gone again.

You've no particular beauty,
just shimmery style,
blithe unconcern,
a joyful ignorance
of where the hook is coming from.

No particular beauty
could not ask for more.

THE MOON IN THE TREE

At five o'clock,
the leafy oak relinquishes detail.
clings to its shape.

The sky behind
is thickening blue to black.
How long can the center hold?

Moon rises,
unseen at first,
but then, where
branch takes leave of trunk,
a yellow crescent shimmers.

Fresh waxing
but shine enough
to ensure the tree
will not be taken from me.

So new moon.
tree-cropped,
wan light fanning out
from elements to whole.

On any night,
more modest aims
inviting my approval.

ADAM'S APPLE

and

BROWN AND CRISPY

and

MUTANT

by

MITCHELL KROCKMALNIK GRABOIS

ADAM'S APPLE

Opera Singer #8 takes the stage for the audition. She has massive breasts that make her head appear comically small. The rest of her torso is a barrel. Her legs are amazingly powerful. I am certain she could win a pulling contest against a pair of Clydesdales or a Massey-Ferguson tractor. Her calves are operatic bowling balls. When she strides away from me to leave the stage, I think of photos of bodybuilders in issues of *Strength and Health Magazine* from the 1950's. Then she is gone and I have not heard a word she has sung.

The next competitor in the opera audition actually is a bodybuilder. I wonder how she manages to fit in the grueling hours of opera and the equally grueling hours with the barbells and the weight machines. The part in her hair is perfect. Do you know how hard it is these days to find a woman with a perfect part? I have studied this.

The last entry in the opera audition is 6'8" tall. He's always wanted to play basketball, but his parents forbade him to associate with the hoi polloi who hung out at the neighborhood courts not far from their deluxe condo tower. Onstage, this young man looks out over the crowd and fantasizes being in a game of three-on-three. An opponent jams him in the Adam's Apple, ruins his voice, and puts an end to his operatic career.

BROWN AND CRISPY

1. I don't want to be an ovenbird. I stare out the thick marred glass of the oven, crane my neck to see through the window above the sink with its borders of stained glass, red roses. I see freebirds sitting on top of the fence, balanced on the cedar pickets. I see mating squirrels chasing each other….

2. It's cool. You're naked, like me. I see your little titties, your little Hannah Montana titties. I see them. I can feel them in my hands. You're naked and licking the head of a sledgehammer. I'm the Sledgehammer (or at least I was). I was the Sledgehammer before I turned into Ovenbird. Now I hardly know who I am.

But here I am, Ovenbird. No mate for me. I'm not going anywhere. My skin is getting brown and crispy. I know life is unfair. But why me? Why must I be the Ovenbird? (Jesus asked the same question, but it was too noisy for anyone to hear it.)

3. Robins have red breasts and eat fat worms. They're in love with life. They have their freedom.

4. I want to be your Sledgehammer, little Hannah, not-so-little-anymore Hannah. Why don't you call my name?

5. Humans say: *Freedom isn't free*, but birds know avian freedom is free. Even ovenbirds, who have no freedom, whose fate is to serve and be served. They don't even thank me for my service. They thank Grandma, but not me. I'm the main event on the platter, all carved up, but do they thank me? No. I'm just the ovenbird.

6. Say my name: Not Heisenberg. *Sledgehammer*.

7. They don't look up and see me in the sky and think: *I wish I could fly*. I'm just the ovenbird, the cause of bloating, belching, indigestion, though they still eat pie afterward and drink coffee.

8. They call me Sledgehammer. Nothing stops me. What I want, I get.

9. Crap. I'm just the ovenbird. Then I'm picked over and done, the ovenbird, without even the sanctuary of an oven, in which to mourn my fate.

10. You hear me? Nothing.

MUTANT

The woman with the dead eyes gave me a sexually transmitted demon. She didn't even have to touch me. She didn't breathe on me. She did it through my laptop screen. The woman with the dead eyes, she's a venereal kitty. She's a human immunodeficiency virus, but she's not human, not really. She's a mutant who keeps mutating. The sum total of her experiences have bashed the humanity out of her.

I didn't click away fast enough. She got me. She gave me a sexually transmitted demon. She's not even pretty. She's ugly. Her ugliness is part of what fascinates me about her. She's an evil scag. All she cares about are the unmet needs of her vagina. She poked me, and it was the beginning of the end.

KAFKA AND THE HAPPINESS MACHINE

and

ON CICADA BROOD XIX

and

SWEET ANGEL, AN AUDITOR

by

KAREN AN-HWEI LEE

KAFKA AND THE HAPPINESS MACHINE

Dear Max—

Is there any invention

as a happiness machine?

With our modern cures for polio

and pox, even the white plague, tuberculosis—

are we still happy, as you say, in unhappiness?

When we toss our bitter shreds of tragedy

and civilization into one gullet,

out of the chute

slides a packet, no, a fragrant satchel of happiness—

dried lavender from the field,

sun-perfumed grass

or strawberries

while the happiness machine,

a sentinel cat or a vendor of knick-knacks,

abolishes the woes of urbanity

in our living room. The day curtains are open.

Max, I can hear your voice, a prayer—

Es war nur ein schöner Traum.

Only a beautiful dream.

ON CICADA BROOD XIX

Prophetic headline—

adult cicadas will fly
in Orange this season.

Broods indexed
by Roman numerals,

wingless nymphs
molted for love-making

every thirteen years.

At dusk, I stroll into
their sleep—
A black eight ball rolls
in darkness. A boy

loosens his tooth
with a shoe horn

as cicadas slumber
in dirt burrows.

High in the trees,
the angle-wing katydid

clicks seven times.

Southern Brood XIX,
a failed prophecy?

Californians cicadas
will emerge in Georgia

and vice versa.

Orange, Georgia.
Orange, California.

Oblivious
to citrus-eyed love,

why does a cicada leave
her shell

for inklings of demise?
Orange

to orange, the light—
southern.

SWEET ANGEL, AN AUDITOR

Gas station with a waterfall mural on the side—
All who are thirsty, come and drink.

A cashier says sweet angel. The other gasps
at my face. You look exactly like the auditor.

Sweet or not, touchless wash-and-wax,
a stranger with my voice audits balance sheets

for cash quirks and tax evasion.
Honestly, I see neither—

bookkeeping skills at bay
while seraphs fly over a megachapel

on fairview avenue,
topaz eyes covered by fire-wings, amused.

Come, all you who are thirsty,
come to the waters....

Come, buy wine and milk without money
and without cost.

NOW UNOBSCURED

by

BRIAN MICHAEL BARBEITO

(NOETIC NOVEMBER AND WALKING THE SIGHT
lines with Emily Dickinson)

I told her that there is not much I could say. I told her that
the ones she might want to talk to, if there were such ones, were
far away and in cities and knew more about books or history. But
then, by some foliage that still remained, having cheated death
for the time being, and some strange faucet affixed to a wall of a
building, I figured I might as well make the most of it and show
her around. For her and I. Emily wore white and her hair was two
moving birds yet still threaded upon themselves like some open
secret.

Quiet but not withdrawn, she followed in step and we went
forward. I must have made a sight in working pants and keys
dangling, almost like a custodian.

Now look, I told her, as we rounded a pathway and then saw
the entrance to a road that needed passing. *I am going to tell you an
odd thing, but it might be the most important thing. And I am going to put it
first. The poetic and noetic, the salvation and living gnosis or the tumultuous
spirit in a sort of trauma due to life itself, are for later, are in fact for you to
codify (the laws of the moderns and such if you shall). I know you to have an
acute consciousness to say the least. What I want you to see is the sight-line. It*

is blocking the traffic and it is dangerous. This is a type of thing that bothers me. Those feral shrubs should be severed. Use them for compost, for fire, for anything—but they are blocking. A soul could wander out from here, to there, and meet with an ending.

So we went and in the going found a light footing. I can't speak for her actually, but I would say so. She had put a sweater over her white dress and though fuller and with proper shoulders, she still looked small. Some spirit that was about her was not, though, and I sensed an eclectic and electrical knowingness. Maybe that was natural for her way and a nonverbal manner of soul. But the world there helped. How so? Well, the November world at dusk in those parts has a sort of wind that comes through the tall grasses. It's, against reason, cold and somehow warm at once. Nobody knows where it comes from. I suppose there could be a lake far off. There are a few, actually, but they are a series and not too large. No, the wind comes as if guided from the invisible yet pronounced astral. It brings a bit of dirt and dusk up, but compared to the feelings it evokes, well, that's nothing at all to worry about. Emily didn't worry. Not that she said so. Not that I saw. She marched right on and we looked all about. Old oaks, frozen against the dimming sky. Some lights blinking on from an old farmer's abode. The earth quaking back behind us from traffic and especially trucks (I think just then she glanced backwards some…) I pointed out the long pathways where the coyotes go across and the coy crescent moon that had announced itself.

We might be able to see Venus, or the North Star, I proclaimed, but I don't remember seeing either.

Carrying on and around a bend, I explained the physical and psychic landscape the best I could. I spoke at a medium pace and tried to be clear.

The field goes in and meets up with another that is lower. Like a

Netherlands field. The paths are at the same time like causeways with nothing on the immediate sides. Now, things are dying or have died but have their own beauty if you can see. You would understand this, no? Slight frost, the old pieces of trees strewn across here and there, solitary, flaxen from the sun, bleached of personality like an old soul, clean and steady and ready for the moon to wash it aglow, to wash it and know. The wind brings itself across from somewhere and has prescience and persistence, but none of the glamour of cities and the secular. It carries something sacrosanct and in-tune, something like a secret that can't really be told but can only be known in another sense. You got it or you don't. Less and less have it. And if I sometimes look upon a tree making its splash against the sky, it is as if the tree is moving impossibly fast in its stillness. And it moves for real in the wind for a moment and is made to shake yet another secret from its limbs. And what is the secret? Well, it is that we are all moribund Emily. Maybe you know that. Surely you do. And at first this makes one to feel aghast or at the least panicky. I mean—my God—our childhood was for this? This November of calendar and also of the calendar of our lives? But in the next moment it's okay. It's okay even though it's not okay. We are going—we are going from here—the trees and the fields shall outlast us and wait for someone else. Maybe I see a rock or a series of rocks, and they are dreaded and distinct and nothing, or maybe I feel the opposite; that the fields are lit up from below, with benevolent lights, the light of existence—and know this can and shall sustain us and all. But whatever is sensed, there is something beyond. And the field can present this. And if you don't go in for that, there is always simply the path and the shrub, the constellations and the night owl or day hawk or red-winged black bird alighting, for instance, on branches in the spring's birth. You can take those things on their own terms and be with them and them alone.

And soon we were coming up around the largest corner of the fields and it was time to think about heading back. I had to say one more thing.

Since all Novembers here are not the same, some are warmer and without snow. If it is late October or early November and it rains, there is a time before the rain. I look with a soft sort of gaze upon a flurry of red and brown leaves on a large tree. These trees have stayed on and the wind tosses and turns them together and it's before a large storm. There is a second or seconds when it is forgotten or else simply not registered that they are leaves on a tree shaken by pre-storm winds. There is instead a mystery and it is felt with intense deepness, incredibly melancholic. So much so, in fact, that death wins. Death is gone into. But it was no death at all. It was life that was really death, and now, in death, paradoxically, one finds life and that one was and is everything. Now unobscured. Do you understand?

I understand.

She did say one thing more. When we were heading back from the fields there was a lot we traversed. Real dark had taken away the dark blue hue from the sky and I tried to glance up at the firmament.

She touched my arm in human concern and said, *Wait.*

I looked down and her gaze was up the way, parallel with the one lane highway but blocked by a tree planted or simply grown independently too close to the traffic's miles:

Watch out for the sight line, said Emily.

IN HER TALONS

by

VICTORIA GRIFFIN

SHE WAS TALL AND SKINNY AS A CANE POLE. I looked up into those coal-gray eyes, sparks flickering beneath the surface, and I bit my tongue when she asked me, "Have you ever loved anyone?"

I couldn't lie, not to her. I felt the veins on my hands popping out as I clenched my fists, and I tucked them into my hoodie so maybe she wouldn't see. We were standing on the dock, the humidity melting us like June snowmen. The lake stretched out in front of us, still and calm, until a hawk dipped its talons into the water and plucked out a fish. The sun reflected off the carp's golden scales, and I thought I could understand what it was feeling. Mary had me in her talons, and I was terrified she would realize she had picked the wrong fish and let me go. The higher she took me, the farther I would fall, but I knew I could never keep her on the ground.

The first time I tried to kiss her, we were parked in my old Chevy outside the empty high school, the spring air breathing through the open windows. The parking lot had already cleared. I'd been in detention, and she'd asked me for a ride home after her volleyball practice let out. I lingered for a moment after starting the car, and when I leaned in for a kiss, I thought the George Strait rolling through the speakers and my hand on her knee would send shivers up her spine, just like every other girl who'd fallen for me.

She didn't even flinch, just left me hanging out over the console like a jackass while she flipped through my CD collection. I ran my fingers through my hair and turned the music up so I wouldn't have to listen to her breathe—it sounded like she was laughing at me. I stretched the speed limit the whole way to her house. She was silent the entire drive. Who did she think she was? I shouldn't let her get to me, I told myself. She was nothing to me—just some girl who wouldn't give it up.

I was headed to my last class on Friday. The days seemed to move more and more slowly as graduation approached. It was already the second semester, and I could feel my feet sinking deeper into the soil of this one-horse town.

I saw Mary strolling toward me through the crowd. Her blond hair curled softly into her face, and her eyes pinned me down before I could think of escaping.

"You change your mind?"

I thought she might float by me before I'd have to answer, but she caught me by the arm and pulled me against the hall's glass windows.

"About what?" I asked.

"Me."

I looked up into her eyes—the only girl who'd ever made my palms sweat. "I don't think I ever made up my mind about you."

She smiled. She knew she had me. She kissed me in the hallway, and her tongue felt like a fish hook piercing my lip.

We were at the senior bonfire when I realized I was in love with her, the first time I understood what it felt like to be afraid. I was sitting on a stump, with her on the ground in front of me, my hands on her shoulders. Our friends were scattered around the fire, faint shadows flickering over the grass, the dark trees looming on the edge of the field. We were all quiet, listening to the night birds and the wood crackling between the fire's jaws.

I couldn't even see Mary's face, but I felt her breathing and realized the danger I had put myself in. She had me, wholly and completely. But Mary was a spirit, a ghost of perfection, and she could never give all of herself to me. I could never ask her to.

I was afraid that if I tried to tie her down, she might just evaporate.

"Have you ever loved anyone?"

I couldn't look at her. I stared out over the darkening lake with my hands stuffed into my hoodie pocket.

"Yes, I have."

She nodded and was quiet.

I waited a moment before asking, "Do you have everything packed?"

"Yes."

I watched the hawk gaining height, its kill lodged in its talons.

"You're going to be great at Vanderbilt. You'll love it."

I kept my gaze away from her, away from those beautiful coal-gray eyes.

"And everyone there will love you."

Stay! Stay! I wanted to beg her, but I couldn't keep her there any more than that fish could ask the hawk to come live beneath the water. The pain of the fall was getting nearer—I'd known it was coming.

"You're going to do something great, Mary. No doubt in my mind."

Her eyes turned on me, shimmering like those of a mermaid just beneath the surface. They reached out, sad and distant, and drew me in like a bucket into a well as she bent her neck to kiss my cheek.

I walked away from that dock loving her more than ever. Mary never did come back from Nashville. I hear she has a kid now—and a man that sticks around on weekends. She's a soccer mom with an I love my poodle bumper sticker.

I'm a fish baking on the dock where I fell from her talons ten years ago, and she's a hawk nesting on the ground in Tennessee.

MUNCY

by

NICK GREGORIO

CLAIRE NEVER WISHED FRANKLIN DEAD. BUT SHE often imagined what life would be like were he to not return home from a shift. What she would do. Where she would go. If she would find out if the issue was her or Franklin. Sometimes Franklin would be late, forget to call and tell her so. She'd sit, watch the television, read a book, bore herself staring at the computer screen in the spare room, then panic until he'd come home.

Lately, Claire had figured that every call that came through was from someone at the station to tell her Franklin had gone and gotten himself killed. Clipped off the side of the road writing a ticket. Stabbed underneath his vest with a buck knife clearing out a fight at the Muncy Pub. Shot through the eye during a standoff down center of town.

But Muncy was mostly drunk drivers running down mailboxes or driving into the front of Metz' tool shed round the blind spot on 83. Breaking and entering. Domestic disputes. Everything else was in bigger towns in bigger counties surrounding bigger cities, places Claire wished she lived. Franklin would tell her so over a beer on good nights—over two, three, four on bad ones.

Regardless, the shift from panic and paranoia to violent fantasy had become permanent. Took root as Claire wanted to tear herself off her own.

With the news talking about more rain, Claire, foggy from her head pills, heard Franklin creak through the screen door on the porch, scrape his boots on the nailed-down mud chucker. She stubbed out her cigarette, sat up on the couch, brushed away the ashes that drifted down the front of her robe.

Franklin stepped in, said hello, then sorry, then he went to the fridge for his beer.

Claire said, "Long night?"

With his head behind the refrigerator door, Franklin said, "Dispute down south end of Cranston's property. Some idiot shot the dog and said he thought it was a bear."

Claire imagined Franklin's obituary were he shot by accident down Cranston's. The wording. The photograph. The term she'd give herself. Widow or wife.

Franklin stood up straight, closed the fridge door. Hanging off one side his face, torn, bloody, showing the white nub of bone, his jaw swung back and forth while he spoke about the type of stupidity it takes to mistake Mr. Cranston's old black lab for a bear.

Then he asked, "What's the matter?" his face mended and whole.

Hand on her chest, mouth open, Claire said, "What?"

"You're looking at me like I grew me a second head."

Claire, stuck in her permanent couch indent, said, "I suppose my mind played a trick on me."

On the television was a report about a homicide far enough away not to matter.

"Well, shit," Franklin said, "Let's watch something other than the damn news then, huh?"

Franklin kissed Claire's cheek, sat beside her in his own ass imprint, turned on something else.

Franklin encouraged Claire every so often to go on out and find something to fill her time with. Told her it's not good having nothing to do but wait home. But most of Claire's friends had children, or had more on the way. They'd looked at her sideways when she'd said she didn't care much for babies. Or the thought of having one. Or the thought of pushing one out of herself. She couldn't very well call them up for a chat. Her single friends had gone and left Muncy all together once it started to fall apart.

Her teaching certificate had expired a few years after the high school closed down. The only other jobs in town—waiting tables at the Soanes' Inn, tending bar at the Muncy Pub—she'd gotten fired from on account of her being damn awful at them and not caring enough to get better.

Franklin's not wanting to leave his home town and Claire's want to get out and go anywhere else had led to daytime television, cigarettes, the shit computer with the lousy DSL, and paperback novels bought from the collapsing supermarket just past the grassed-over railroad tracks.

Claire took the last of her pills, spent the morning writing letters to Franklin. Letters about how unhappy she was living in a ghost town. Letters about her love for him not being enough to continue living the way she was. Letters about the things she'd been keeping from him.

She balled them all up, took them out back and burned them. Figured it'd be better not to destroy Franklin with just her chicken scratch.

She drove miles out of town, down the highway, past the rusted empty factories, through a tunnel until a city rose up from the horizon.

Driving, she practiced what she was going to say over the

phone whenever she stopped wherever she was headed.

"Frank, I want a divorce—no—Franky, I need a divorce—no—You're a wonderful man, Frank, but I'm…goddammit."

She thought of his face, red and melting in grief.

She thought of the sounds he would make, wet sobbing and whimpers.

She thought of him killing himself, putting his gun in his mouth.

The car drifted over a rumble strip, but Claire jerked the wheel left just before she got the chance to slam into a bridge abutment.

Further down the highway she drafted a big rig, could read the registration sticker on the license plate, waited for brake lights, waited for her car to cram itself underneath the tires.

She imagined plowing through the cement wall on the bridge past Stanton, the car nose-diving into the valley, exploding when it hit.

Instead, she eased the car off the highway at the next exit, made her way back to the on-ramp and headed on back toward Muncy. The only one who would care if she'd gone and died would be that poor dumb boy, Franklin. And he didn't deserve that.

She regretted thinking him dumb. Simple and happy, he deserved the kindnesses he'd given.

She decided to run the errands she'd planned on never running again.

At her last stop, a pharmacy just outside Dunlop, the pharmacist smiled at her, said hello.

Claire did the same, said, "How you been?"

"Same ol', same ol', you know? No one ever told me life would be so boring."

"Could be worse, I suppose."

"Could be, sure. Boring job. You know how it goes."

Claire said nothing.

"But sometimes I think quitting would be nice."

Claire asked for her prescriptions.

The pharmacist went to the back, pulled two noisy white paper bags from the shelf, handed them over to her.

Claire gave a shot at a smile, but turned, said thanks and left. She drove home and waited for Franklin's shift to end.

Franklin came home early, asked Claire if she wanted to try again.

Afterward, Claire showered, took her pills—one for her brain, one for her lady parts—and hid them deep down in her otherwise useless travel kit. Then she went back to the bedroom to find Franklin still nude, sleeping on top of the covers.

She watched him a bit. His chest rising, falling, his breaths turning into snotty snoring.

He'd left his work clothes on the floor next to the bed. His duty rig and gun at the top of the heap instead of hanging from the doorknob where he usually left them.

He was a sweet man. Dopey. A little chubby. But kind, funny. He liked how much Claire read, told her so back when they first were married. He'd said marrying a smart woman made him feel smarter. He was never smart. He only knew things he knew and everything else was Claire's territory.

But Claire couldn't call herself smart. Not anymore.

She imagined coming home from a job she liked, from a job that don't exist, finding Franklin on the bed, riddled with bullet holes. Someone he had once put away had been released from prison, went to find him, murdered him in his sleep. Unloaded

Franklin's own service weapon into his chest, gut, and balls.

Franklin farted, woke himself up.

He scratched his belly, blinked sleep away, said, "Honey?"

"Just getting up to shower."

Franklin said okay, turned over and quickly fell back to sleep.

Claire smoked cigarettes and drank Franklin's beer until she fell asleep on the couch.

Varied and increasingly grisly fantasies of Franklin's end drove Claire to flush her Effexor down the shitter. Then she stopped going to her therapist after she couldn't bring herself to tell him that Franklin's death was occupying most of her waking thoughts. And her dreams. And when she wasn't thinking of Franklin dying she was thinking of drowning herself. Shooting herself. Setting herself on fire.

During her last session, Claire had said she felt the medication was doing something funny to her. That it was making her feel awful things about Franklin who had never done nothing to her but let her settle into boredom and depression—not that it was ever his responsibility.

She'd said, "I don't exist."

Said, "I'm nothing."

Said, "Nobody would notice if I just up and left."

Her therapist asked, "Why not just leave then, Claire? Start over if you're so unhappy?"

"I can't. Franklin's a good man. Doesn't deserve that kind of pain."

"Then you need to let the medicine do its job—which takes time—or you need to get up the courage to change."

Claire hadn't been back since.

She took long drives most days after that. One day she went

so far she got home later than Franklin.

He asked where she'd gone when she got home, the back of his skull gone, chunks of brain slopping down onto the couch as he spoke.

Her eyes stung. She blinked away tears. Then said, "I'm trying to get myself something to do."

"Well, then, I think that's great. But leave a note for me next time, okay? Damn scared me half to death."

Claire sat next to Franklin, lit a cigarette. She started to cry. Nearly lit her hair on fire, cigarette still pinched between her fingers.

Franklin wrapped his arm around her shoulders, asked what was wrong. Said he can't do anything to help if she won't tell him what's got her all spun about. Said she needs to calm down so they can talk.

Claire wept longer than she thought she needed to. Wondered if it was genuine, or some deep down intention to lie.

Franklin asked, "What is it, Claire? What's going on?"

Claire sucked back on her runny nose, couldn't think of anything to say, but said, "I want a baby, Frank. I want a baby so bad."

"Maybe we should try and talk to one of them baby doctors?"

"Maybe." Claire took Franklin's hand, stood, led him into the bedroom.

Their appointment with the specialist was set for a week from Wednesday. During the week leading up to it, Claire kept taking her pill. Kept venturing further away from Muncy every day. Kept bedding Franklin to make up for almost not coming home most days.

But she started drinking up most of the beer in the house.

Sick and guilty by day, drunk and horny by night, Claire got careless. Left lit cigarettes in the ashtray until they were nothing but a butt and a straw of gray dust. Misplaced things. Neglected things. Microwaved old frozen dinners. Used tissues in place of the toilet paper she neglected to buy when she was out every day.

The Monday before the appointment she walked down to the Muncy Pub, sat, drank, and waited for someone to say hello. She drank until she stood, said, "None of you motherfuckers would miss me if I left, huh?"

They asked her real nice to leave.

Tuesday she drove straight through two counties, planned not to go back, for sure this time.

She did ninety most the way down the highway hoping for a tire to blow and flip the car. Or a deer to jump out onto the road and send her flying through the windshield. Or a piece of rebar to break loose from a truck hauling bundles of the stuff and impale her through the mouth, out the back of her head.

She pulled over hyperventilating, crying, thinking of Franklin getting home to an empty house, waiting for her to come home, sitting there until he died, rotted, turned to dust.

If she was going to leave him she'd at least tell him to his face. Kind, but honest. Maybe give him the option to come with her. But she was leaving with or without him. She practiced her speech all the way home to keep from turning to chickenshit.

She got home after dark. After Franklin.

He'd left all the lights on. Left the television on. Left a trail of beer cans from the coffee table to the armchair to the bedroom.

The bedroom door was open a crack from the weight of Franklin's rig hanging from the doorknob on the other side.

Lit by the lights from the living room, lying on the bed, Franklin laid on his back in spilt beer, the overturned empty can next to his hand.

Claire said, "Frank."

He didn't move.

Claire wondered if he'd drunk himself to death.

He scratched his belly.

Claire almost reached to shake him awake, almost said she had something she needed to talk with him about.

Then she saw the blister pack of her pills on the end table.

She imagined him finding them. Using the computer in the spare room to look up the brand name. Crying. Drinking. Passing out drunk as piss, wrecked, betrayed.

Claire backed into the door, heard Franklin's gun clunk against the wood.

Crying, she reached for the pistol, pulled it from the holster.

She cocked the gun, put the barrel in her mouth, tasted the metal and oil.

He'd find her, blame himself. He'd resent her, hate himself for it. He'd live alone, die alone, get found because of the smell.

Claire pulled the gun barrel from between her teeth.

She walked toward Franklin.

His mouth open, snoring, Claire cried for him. Regretted lying to the dimwit. Regretted marrying the fool.

She aimed the gun at his face.

Then she pulled the trigger.

She watched Franklin's brains spray down her pillow, a clump of hair, blood and bone flop onto the headboard.

Claire took Franklin's rig with her. She loaded her car with things she thought she'd need. Ignored the neighbor across the creek asking what had happened. She cried again pulling away from the house, but knew Franklin was better now not having to know everything she'd felt. She drove past the Soane's Inn, the

Muncy Pub, the police station, and clear out of Muncy. She left the county, crossed into another, drove through a tunnel. There was red and blue in her rearview, but a city was on the horizon, lit up and blocking out the stars.

UNTIL IT FEELS REAL

by

CHRISTINE BETTIS

IT IS ALREADY SO HOT.

I've bought berries and frozen berries. *Do these bright colors have their own autonomy or generative power*? Maybe.

There are 74 ways to conjugate 'to forget' in English. To internalize? I don't know.

Roaches have been visiting me. They could be news.

I keep medical graphs folded in Bhanu Kapil's *Ban en Banlieue*. My bed should be made when I read them.

Her skin is sexy glass and I: also a transparent animal but in jellied skin, at the bottom of the pool on a sunny day. There is a breeze. Sun scales multiply, mature, and then exist as something else at the bottom of the pool. One of a hunk of jellied skin, thrown into the pool and sinking down to the bottom. That sinking skin-shape as watery glitter ghost. It would brush up against the back of your leg. You would take it in your hands and masticate it, wanting berry pulp.

Tell me what you need. A cup of water? A big fucking car? *The transformative element*? Notice chlorine's visceral existence in the atmosphere. Chlorine is very tender. Wet, it's heavy and near tears. It's on you.

Episodic lawns connect to the same wire. I throw myself into the circuit. Can I be a leaf, in green fur, almost homemade.

A PAIR OF GUMSHOES IN CAFÉ KAKAO

and

ERATOSTHENES OF CYRENE

and

CAULROPHOBIA

by

JIM DAVIS

A PAIR OF GUMSHOES IN CAFÉ KAKAO

Oklahoma City, OK

Red Detective said I'm edgy, should have

ordered bacon, the sausage stinks of incense.

Blue eyes brim with what they've seen: head

dress, feather, forensic nuance. For instance,

on site at the museum, Red turned & tugged

his partner's blazer, pointed to a tree—

it's a yellow throated vireo, he said

& partner Green said no it's a phoenix—

they stared at each other for a moment

which turned into hours, each refusing

to forfeit the silent contest. It grew dark

in the clearing where the son confessed

the secret sausage ingredient. Bones in

the floor belong to a toll collector named Ben.

ERATOSTHENES OF CYRENE

With a little more than string & a bob

you can take the pulse of the planet.

Comparing the shadow length of cattails

in Alexandria & Syrene, Eratosthenes

tick-tocked the turning of earth

with homemade pendulums & time

enough to chew rounds of emmer

wheat by the river where a great white

stork landed, spirited rings & shook.

Spring reeds bend like sieves of prime

equations in Egyptian wind which blew

a soft cap from the head of his teacher,

Zeno, who he couldn't approach, since

together they unwound the stoic fires.

CAULROPHOBIA

Blinko & Natalya in a blizzard, red

rubber nose on the dresser, reflected

in glass spectacles of polished sand,

like time falling through thick leisure

of brandies by the fire as snow buries

the entryway. Candles waver. She

cannot stay here without tonguing

the stale air. He rewinds the tape

to watch a woman pouring water,

removes his makeup slowly, unbuttons

soft buttons. Caged behind the trailer,

the bear balances on a red rubber ball,

smells of black fish, entranced by her

first glimpse of heavy falling snow.

TECTONIC HEART

by

STAR SPIDER

THERE'S SOMETHING TO THIS PLACE, SHE SAID. *It makes me believe in transformation.*

She leaned up against the glass and it reflected her whole body back into the world, skipping her image like a flat rock across the still pond beside her.

I feel if I sit still enough I'll just become a part of the earth, my ribs tectonic plates, my heart the viscous molten core.

That would hurt, he replied.

She laughed and folded herself into an imitation of the volcanic hills beyond.

It would be peaceful, moving so slowly that time stretches out and your days become millennia.

I'd get bored, he said.

No, because your mind would be geological. You wouldn't feel in the same way a human does. Everything would be petrified by stone and age, sharp pains would be slow tickles.

She rearranged herself again, forehead resting on her knees. She breathed,

    in,

            out,

           in,

                out.

I'd rather be a bird, he said. *Fly high and dive swiftly*.

She looked up to see a bird of prey, a distant pale dot reflecting off the water, the glass. Every image there was an echo, rippling into silence. She glanced over at him but she didn't want to look. His luminous delicacy disturbed her, made her want to reach out but there was nothing to touch.

You're too thin, she said. *They should feed you better*.

You should feed yourself, too, he whispered, but she didn't hear him because his voice was lost to a sudden breeze.

No, you're right. I want to be a bird too.

She sat up straight and stuck her feet out in front of her like two support beams made of flesh and marrow.

I want to fly to the edge of the atmosphere and just let myself drop. Down and down and down forever, right into the centre of the earth.

Bullshit, he said. *You'd never let yourself go like that.*

I could!

Prove it.

How?

Let me go.

The silence settled in, all the images no longer echoes but static things; heavy, immutable. Even the ashen bird froze in the sky. The wind hushed in deep respect. The land held its breath to listen.

The door to the conference centre swung open silently and a group of writers marched out, men and women, haggard but pleased. They huddled in a cluster and lit cigarettes, the bright red tips like cartoon exaggerations.

Hey, one of the men said.

Hey, she replied.

Who were you talking to?

He left his smoke in his mouth and it dulled the edges of his words.

She was silent for another moment, her reflection tense against the glass.

Nobody, she replied.

Just came out here to get away?

She looked over to where her companion's image had been and felt her tectonic heart shift. No echo of him remained.

I was thinking of transforming into a bird, she said.

That would make a good story, the man replied.

Yeah, maybe it would.

ESCAPIST

and

AT THE MINOR PROPHET'S POKER GAME

and

LATE SONATA

by

MARK J. MITCHELL

ESCAPIST

He did not really expect to escape:

His tunnel wound through the graveyard, veered left

then dropped through broken catacombs. His next

untrick was carving words into gunshapes

then taking a shower, but nothing came

of that. At least he was clean. He stacked time

in locked closets for bribes but no one came

with a hand held out. He tried to design

windows with his remembered pencil dipped

in snow. They melted, leaving messy lines

that might spell out last names of unfrocked saints.

His guards would come back, he knew, and they'd paint

the walls khaki—again. He didn't mind

as long as they left the ghost of her lips.

AT THE MINOR PROPHET'S POKER GAME

Jonah passes on sushi

while Hosea complains

endlessly about his wife.

Habakkuk shuffles

the cards but Joel

is too angry to cut them.

Nahum seeks the comfort

of Abishag the Shunemite.

Haggai and Malachi

draw two cards each and

Micah walks humbly from the room

leaving all his cash on the table.

LATE SONATA

The sad girl with a lipstick smear,

crying soft, just under my dream,

is a stranger. Her odd, dry tears

leave make-up intact, so it seems.

Anyway, there are no dark streams

of black mascara from her eyes.

I don't know what her presence means,

just some quite nocturnal lie.

Because the dream's not about her. I

am playing the piano and am near

a tricky bridge. The music sighs,

carries me with it as I smear

the air with sharp sounds—not quite clear.

Suddenly a light, a focused beam

falls on E-flat. Notes become tears.

A wonder: A girl gets seen.

FIVE DRAWINGS

by

ALLEN FORREST

"Adopted Family"

"Designing"

"From the Good Ol' Days"

"Interlude"

"Little Things"

THROUGH THE WINDOW

by

CONNOR WOOD

WHERE US 6 AND NEVADA 375 MEET IS A HOUSE THAT visited me on those autumn evenings when the sky is sharp and there's almost a chill in the air. It sits alone at a desert crossroads: just two rooms, white walls with peeling blue trim, no windowpanes or doors. Beer cans, shotgun shells, and the detritus of the transient lie in dunes on the floor; cryptic writings cover the walls. Out the hollow windows I can see empty roads stretching away in three directions.

I've been there just once.

It visited me also in the dead heat of certain afternoons when the light outside is so bright that no bulb can compete and everything tastes like ash. I shuffle through the ruins, not quite alone; the pilgrims and pariahs have wandered on to other haunts and in their wake is the eerie suggestion that there is nothing to keep me from their paths. I suspect that I am the only reason I don't just start for that wavering horizon. That nothing is fixed. That faith, fate, and freedom aren't all that different.

For two years I stared out the empty eyes of the house at a desolate horizon rimmed in broken glass, uneasy and unable to look away. It visited me more and more, heavy with adumbrations of forgotten lines, of missed cues. I spent whole nights there waiting for the AC to click on and interrupt the calls of imagined owls or drown out the howl of imagined winds. I spent blinks there, the entire place roaring in as my eyelids shut, complete to the last cobweb, demanding without urgency or pity a response. But I tended bar and slept until noon and knew some day I'd die. I had nothing to say.

I told some friends that I was haunted by a house, which got a good laugh, which made me smile, but didn't resolve anything. I told them I was going to visit the place and they told me to bring spare batteries for my Specter Detector, which got a good laugh. Three days later I left town.

The road led north and along it I sped, out across a wide basin where yellow earth wavered in the heat as dust devils scurried like a plague of eels—fevered motion below pale palisades and an empty blue sky. Across another through plumes of salt and earth whipped into diaphanous sheets of white fire. Waves of blue mountains against a deepening yellow sky and still the road led on. I saw the first stars and the looming yellow moon burning against the indigo night, and I stopped.

The earth was tearing itself apart and building itself up without haste or pretense. The plates stretch and break and along those thousand faults the pieces were tipping, one end sinking into the furnaces, the other rising up from the desert. Row after row of mountains and between them, planed by wind and water and time, basin after basin. It was not a veil for other things, it was all. Stillness reigned, not silence or stasis, but a vast and eviscerating repose. I stood alone on the gravel roadside.

I saw then in the distance orange lights darting across the sky. I squinted and for a moment there was nothing. Then again, orange lights appearing and disappearing. Then slowly the stars in that sector of night returned. Then another arc of orange fire. In the solitude of some other basin behind barbed wire and armed guard, the government was shooting at stars.

The guys launching the rockets must have raging erections, pressing buttons to summon fiery death—twenty psi from the right index finger for twenty megatons, a good trade. But they were too close, too close. They saw the white flash and felt the launch deep in their chests and knew on an intellectual level that it was just a test but understood also that it was not a test, never a test. All that light and sound and motion must be real, must be right. (Right? they wonder sometimes, alone behind closed doors.)

But from here: just tiny orange arcs in a riot of stars so distant that their ancient light could be that of a burned out husk. And even if it was, or if some tested missile found its mark, the sky would be no darker. The universe expands, the mountains rise and fall like waves in a stony sea, the stillness remains, I am adrift.

It had watched impassive as I bustled about the city, drunk on inchoate notions of my own importance. The lights of dreams, the sounds of promises, the empty gestures: hurry, hurry, scurry, worry, and gaze not deeply into the mirror. Live for who you might be at the small cost of who you are, because you don't miss what you never knew. Frenetic days, passed under entropy's burgeoning shadow. I was swept along by the sense that something would happen, and things did happen, but never the elusive event that would....

I'd been too close, and seeing it from here, it hadn't all been nothing, but it hadn't been much more than reflex.

And I understood that all along the house was insisting on distance, although I'd felt it backwards.

And I was there. I was there but this time I wasn't looking out, the world was looking in. The windows were microscope slides and I a microbe. The vast barren horizon and behind it a maelstrom of mileyears, each an inevitable transect trailing some unborn juncture at which, whatever the means, I would turn forever, all of it gazed unblinking through the window at me. I stared in anguish down the barrel of that Gordian future certain then that I could follow any of them, that the only question was which it would be. I was a point anchoring infinite vectors, a sphere whose radius is precisely death.

So I am condemned to choose, will become that choice, will forever be choosing, forever creating myself. I'll spiral like sparks or warheads towards stars I'll never reach, squirming across glass under a withering light, but free.

Volition is a crown, not a yoke. I will visit the house, and smile.

WINTER HOMECOMING

and

FALL

by

LIZ PURVIS

WINTER HOMECOMING

I forgot how much I'd missed the stars. Coming home
after a long time gone, the look up at country sky

feels both familiar and wild. On the right
clear night, I can find Orion, Ursa Major,

Cassiopeia and her husband his name lost
from my memory, still wedged somewhere in old books.

I couldn't see the stars in London, where I'd wanted
to share them, to find the ones I know tri-studded belt, crooked

tail, crown and point them out to a man
who, between incessant clouds and high, bright lights,

hardly had the chance to see. That fantasy is gone
now, like an archer fades from summer sky

or a love we both said wouldn't end. So I returned
to hills I knew, left plate-glass buildings for brick storefronts,

went back to see pin-pricks in darkness rather than
reflections, the wide-eyed city's endless light—

instead, I watched stars come out alone
from the wooden porch, the tree-lined yard.

FALL

Mornings, I watch leaves
drop from the pin oak, watch

how the breeze sends them twirling
off my porch's frame through steam

rising off coffee. There's a man I don't love
in my shower, rinsing last night from his skin.

I did that already. My wet hair drapes
its shawl around my shoulders, traces

cool, light shadows down my spine.
When he comes out, clothed, steps

into the room still rubbing
my towel over his head, I will offer him

eggs, some toast, my squat mug's twin.
If he wants to, I might even

let him fill the seat, briefly, sit warm
beside me; I might let him rest

his hand on the crook of my leg, might
tilt my damp head for a moment

toward his— let him watch with me

the leaves as they fall

in the wind, every last possible one.

RESEARCH

by

TOM LARSEN

CATCH A RIDE OUTSIDE OF DALLAS. GARY; LEXUS; Florida tags. Gary's bound for Vegas and he's ripped on something–speed, by the sound of it. Wouldn't be a stretch to say the highways run on amphetamines. He goes on forever about his car wreck, his DUI and his gambling problem. Mostly he talks about his wife, Stupid Bitch.

"The stupid bitch blows in like a tsunami, BOOM, table goes one way, chips go the other. I'm holding three kings with a thumb up my ass! OOH, but when I'm on a roll you don't hear a peep. Money can buy some peace and quiet, I can assure you."

Gary likes to assure me of things. So far I have his assurance that the Rangers suck, the Cowboys suck, money makes money and Angelina Jolie's tits are real. How he knows the last is what I want to know.

"Stupid bitch finds out I tapped the college fund and goes ballistic!" he waves his hands. "My kid is three! When you feel it you go for it, fuck the college fund. Sorry, that's the way I am. She knew that going in, stupid bitch."

Gary stops a few times for I know what and a cell phone call. Whoever he's plaguing doesn't answer—caller ID, a wonderful thing. After the last stop he comes back a mess.

"You all right?" I have to ask.

"Sure," he just sits there. "I'm broke, I'm sick and my wife just left me. I'm fucking great!"

Christ, what do you say to that? In the first place it's none of my business and in the second, I'm pulling for the stupid bitch.

"Sick?"

"At heart."

"Maybe if I drive."

"Stupid bitch," Gary blubbers.

"Come on, switch seats," I pop my seatbelt. "You can rest. It's rough, I know."

His eyes cut over.

"What do you care? You don't even know me."

"You picked me up. I owe you," I force a smile. "You wanna talk? I'll listen. Put on some miles, it'll do you good."

We switch. He talks.

"I've known Jeanette since the seventh grade. We got married in high school. Can you believe it? Hell, I would have married any girl who'd fuck me. High school, can you imagine? You don't even know who you are yet!"

Nice car. It occurs to me that in my six decades I've never owned a nice car, or even a new car. My wife sprang for a Beetle when they came back out but I rarely drive it. My own car is a twelve-year old station wagon with a hubcap missing and a check-engine light that's always on.

"I mean what do you know in high school? Nothing." Gary rolls his head against the headrest. "If you could see the kid you were in tenth grade you'd cringe. Things you thought were important weren't important and people you thought were cool weren't cool. I just learned how to drive and now I'm getting *married*? You know who does that? An idiot does that. First class, I can assure you."

"It works for some."

"You know who it works for?" his head rolls my way. "People who peak in tenth grade. You can see the ones, 18 going on 50, the nobodies who know it."

"Yeah, well...."

The thing about luxury cars: the luxury. I suppose you get used to it but I don't see how.

"A guy your age—how many times have you been divorced?"

"I've never been divorced," I level with him.

"Never?"

"Married twenty-five years." I smile to think. "I've known my wife since we were kids."

He waves me off. "You could tell me anything. How would I know?"

"You wouldn't, but it's true. The difference is I was over thirty when I got married."

Gary thinks about that while I lock on the fast lane.

"So...that's the way you planned it? You said to yourself, 'I'm not getting married until I'm thirty'?"

"No, not like that. It wasn't really an issue."

Push it to ninety, smooth as silk. Gary doesn't seem to notice.

"It was my idea," he tells me. "My wife, Jeanette, is a piece of work. Type triple A with a face and body to match. I couldn't let anyone come between us and I thought marrying her would be the way. Can you imagine that?"

"You were a kid."

"So how come I'd do it again?"

I cut inside on a long banked curve. Not much traffic so I goose it to triple digits.

"So, you love her, right?"

"From the neck down. I had a dream once where I could unscrew her head," he laughs. "That was a good dream."

Cruising at 120, the road unwinds like a video game. Lexus—nice—if I could afford one I wouldn't get one. The thing about luxury: it makes me nervous. A nice car would mean too much to me. I'd obsess. Better to have a car you don't care about. I don't give a rat's ass about the station wagon.

"Happily married, what a crock!" Gary snorts. "So what are you doing scuffling?"

I tell him the truth and I have to admit it sounds pretty wifty.

"So, you're a writer," he bobs his head. "You've been published?"

"Not so you'd notice."

"Another road book. Good luck with that."

I give him a look. His head keeps bobbing.

"Anything memorable happen so far?"

"Depends on what you mean by memorable. Strangers confined together, it's a unique situation. Somehow it always makes an impression."

"I bet this never happened before," Gary nods to the small handgun cradled in his lap. I ease off the gas as my limbs stiffen.

"What's that for?"

"Plan B."

"...what's plan A?"

He smiles and shakes his head.

"You'll laugh."

"I won't. I assure you."

"When I get to Vegas I'm going to put everything I've got on a roll of the dice. One roll, all or nothing."

"And if you lose?"

Gary puts the gun to his head.

"…and if you win?"

He scratches his head with the barrel.

"I haven't given it much thought. I mean what are the chances?"

"You said you were broke."

Gary reaches in his pocket and pulls out a necklace—diamonds, looks like. He holds it to the light.

"I paid twenty grand and the stupid bitch refused to wear it. Said it's too gaudy."

Guns and diamonds in Iowa, right?

"Put the gun away, okay?"

But instead he starts to play with it, twirling it on his finger, spinning the bullet thing. It sounds just like a gun on TV.

"This will make a good chapter."

He cocks the hammer.

"Crazy guy with a death wish, definitely not the ride you were after. I mean, who knows, I might just shoot you."

I grip the wheel to keep my hands from shaking.

"Why would you do that?"

He shrugs.

"I don't know. Irrational people do irrational things."

I take a chance.

"You're not irrational. You're just feeling sorry for yourself."

Gary smacks his lips. "Or you might piss me off."

So here it is. If Gary's half the flake I think he is I'm in a world of trouble here. I don't think he's revved up enough to shoot me…yet. But we're a full day from Vegas and he's bound to keep cranking. Whatever happens will be messy and exhausting.

"Why don't we stop somewhere, get something to eat?"

I nod to a cluster of rest stop signs.

"Just keep driving."

He pockets the necklace and folds his arms, gun pointed my way. I think about how it will hurt, the organs involved, the closest hospital. Gary bobs his head to the radio, white guys rapping.

"You're thinking about it, aren't you?"

He snickers.

"The way you'd write it."

"I'm thinking about my liver."

"You're 55 years old."

He does the math.

"Ever think maybe you missed the writing boat?"

"You mind if I smoke?"

"Please do. What's secondhand smoke to a man with two plans? Hey, there's a line for you," he says, jabbing me with the fucking thing. "About that boat. What do you think?"

So maybe I am writing it in my head. In that case I want to get this right. I want to say what someone who gets out of this would say.

"I think you're making a mistake."

I manage a shrug.

"In ten years you'll be so involved in something else you'll have trouble remembering this. Who knows, you could be happy. Be a shame to miss *that* boat."

He mouths my words, bobbing and grinning. A well-placed elbow to the nose might do it.

"Ten years ago *you* were in the same boat," he says. "Same wife, same delusion, failed writer hacking away."

Maybe stomp the brakes, bounce him off the dash. But, of course, then he'd have a reason to shoot me.

"Same wife. The rest is different," I tell him.

"Thing is, I've tried to live without her. It doesn't work. I make myself sick wondering what she's doing and who she's doing it with. I can't stop and I can't do it anymore."

"Okay, fair enough."

I keep my eyes on the road.

"It's your life, but what about me? I've got nothing to do with any of it."

"Don't start sniveling," he says, waving the gun. "I hate a fucking sniveler."

"That's not sniveling. That's just a question."

"Look," Gary slides around to face me. "I haven't decided what I'm gonna do yet so back off. You don't want to force my hand."

"You're running the show?"

"That's right. I am."

"Only you're facing some major felonies should you have, you know, a change of heart."

Please, God, rip out my tongue.

"Maybe that's the whole point," Gary whispers. "Paring down the old options. Of course I could never do the time."

The whisper, very creepy, and the saliva paste—Jesus!

I keep my voice steady.

"No problem there. You put the gun away and I forget it ever happened."

"Really. That's awful nice of you,…Tom, was it?"

"That's right. I'll even drive you to Vegas and check you in."

"You know what? Let's do it."

He puts the gun in his pocket. Could it be that easy? I hold a few beats then sneak a peek over.

"So, we're okay?"

The gun comes back out again.

"I like it better this way, dramatic tension and all that. Gives me an edge."

Past El Paso we get a flat and Gary makes me change it. Lexus, right? I take as long as I can, but who stops to help the rich guy? What would I do anyway, drag someone else into it? Back on the road Gary tells me about his daughter, Melanie. Shows me her picture, cute kid, whatever. His cell phone rings every now and then, post time bugle call, fucking handjob. He checks the ID but doesn't answer.

"I took Melanie to the track on her third birthday."

He snorts a laugh.

"She bet the six horse, the red one she called it. Went off the long shot and won going away, 60 to 1, the freaking red horse. You a betting man, Tom?"

"Not so much."

"Poker's my game, or was," he taps his chin with the gun. "Then one night I'm in AC and I got a bluff going. The bluff is my thing, right? I mean to win when you shouldn't, to psyche the guy, that's what does it for me. And this bozo is sweating bullets. Frat fuck, big mouth, I mean I really want this guy. So I put on my game face and raise him a grand, only something's wrong with my game face. My right eye, I can feel it twitching. Not so you'd notice unless you were looking, but everybody *was* looking. There's a couple of grand on the table and it's all eyes on me! *Twitching*!"

"It's only nerves," I tell him. "It could mean anything."

"In real life, maybe. But in poker it means you're bluffing. End of story I can assure you."

"Does it still twitch?"

"Only when I'm playing poker," Gary points to his head. "It's in here."

"You could fake it. Throw them off."

"I tried that, but the slick ones can differentiate."

"You could wear dark glasses."

"No good. You can still see it."

Like I give a rat's ass. And where's a cop when you need one? Not that I would try anything. If Gary shoots me we'll likely crash. Either would be bad but both would be twice as bad.

"So it's craps."

He gives me a wink.

"One roll—all or nothing."

We pass the exit for the University of Texas. Way back when I would stop and hit the dorms for a shower and a meal. Blending in might be a problem these days but the mid point reference appeals to me. I'm thinking Gary wouldn't go for it.

"I want you to be honest with me."

He pulls out the necklace again.

"Would you say this is gaudy?"

I'm no expert but gaudy nails it.

"It's…nice."

"Nice?"

He spins it on his finger.

"Flowers are nice. Candy is nice. We're talking twenty large!"

"Hey, what do I know?"

"Nothing."

He lets fly and the necklace clatters against the dash.

"You don't know jack-shit!"

"Okay."

"Shut the fuck up," he barks.

So I do.

Cattle country, but we don't see it. He's too wrapped up in the gun and the advantage and I'm too busy beaming compliance. The miles pile up and the tension takes a toll. My mouth tastes like metal, I need to eat and I'm sensing Gary doesn't like me anymore.

I break the silence.

"We'll need to gas up pretty soon."

"So…do it."

The rest stop has a hundred pumps, three of them occupied. I pull up close to the pay booth. A billion bugs swirl in the vapor light.

"Well?"

Gary fingers the necklace.

"You pump it. I'm not going out there."

I push out the door and start walking.

GRANT CURRIER lives in Ohio, where he earned his MFA, and now works as an English teacher.

JOHN GREY is an Australian poet, US resident. Recently published in *New Plains Review*, *Big Muddy* and *Spindrift* with work upcoming in *South Carolina Review*, *Gargoyle*, *Sanskrit* and *Louisiana Literature*.

MITCHELL KROCKMALNIK GRABOIS has had over eight hundred of his poems and fictions appear in literary magazines in the U.S. and abroad. He has been nominated for the Pushcart Prize for work published in 2012, 2013, and 2014. His novel, *Two-Headed Dog*, based on his work as a clinical psychologist in a state hospital, is available for Kindle and Nook, or as a print edition. He lives in Denver.

KAREN AN-HWEI LEE is the author of *Phyla of Joy* (Tupelo, 2012), *Ardor* (Tupelo, 2008), and *In Medias Res* (Sarabande, 2004), winner of the Kathryn A. Morton Prize and the Norma Farber First Book Award from the Poetry Society of America. A book of literary criticism, *Anglophone Literatures in the Asian Diaspora* (Cambria, 2013), was selected for the Cambria Sinophone World Series. Lee's work appears in journals such as *The American Poet*, *Poetry*, *Kenyon Review*, *Journal of Feminist Studies & Religion*, *Iowa Review*, and *IMAGE: Art, Faith, & Mystery*, and she was recognized by the Prairie Schooner/Glenna Luschei Award. The recipient of an NEA Fellowship, Lee currently serves as full professor of English and chair at a liberal arts college in greater Los Angeles. She holds an MFA from the Program in Literary Arts at Brown University and a PhD in British & American Literature from the University of California, Berkeley.

BRIAN MICHAEL BARBEITO is the author of *Chalk Lines*, (Fowlpox Press, 2013, cover art and design by Virgil Kay). Recent work appears at *CV2 The Canadian Journal of Poetry and Critical Writing*, and is forthcoming at *Fiction International*.

VICTORIA GRIFFIN's short fiction has appeared in *Calliope Nerve*, the *Fringe Magazine*, *Fiction 365*, *6 Tales*, and *The Lyricist*, and is forthcoming in *Apeiron Review* and *Down in the Dirt Magazine*.

NICK GREGORIO lives, writes, and teaches in Philadelphia. His fiction has appeared in *Maudlin House*, *Crack the Spine*, *Yellow Chair Review* and more. He is a staff writer and assistant editor for the arts and culture blog, *Spectrum Culture*, and currently serves as a fiction editor for *Driftwood Press*. He earned his MFA from Arcadia University in May 2015 and has fiction forthcoming in *The Bitchin' Kitsch*. Nick is currently hard at work shopping/revising/rewriting his first novel. He also writes, plays guitar, and sings for a Philadelphia punk rock band.
http://www.nickgregorio.com/

CHRISTINE BETTIS is a poet from Detroit and this fall she'll be a second year MFA candidate at UNLV. Her work has appeared or is forthcoming in *Two Serious Ladies*; *Queen Mob's Tea House*; *Storm Cellar*; and *Action*. Yes, she's currently working on a dank/chthonic epic poem. Tweet to her: @poetlump or
email her: bettischristine@gmail.com.

JIM DAVIS is a Master's candidate at Harvard University, and has previously studied at Northwestern University and Knox College. His work has appeared in *Seneca Review*, *Santa Clara Review*, *Sugar House Review*, *Midwest Quarterly*, and *California Journal of Poetics*, among many others. In addition to the arts, Jim is a teacher, coach, and international semi-professional football player.

STAR SPIDER is a writer from Toronto, Canada where she lives and works with her awesome husband Ben Badger. Star is super excited for the publication of her debut novel, which is coming soon! Star's short stories can be found in many places including *A cappella Zoo*, *Necessary Fiction*, *Flyleaf Journal*, *Gone Lawn*, *Maudlin House* and *Klipspringer Magazine*. starspider.ca

MARK J. MITCHELL studied writing at UC Santa Cruz under Raymond Carver, George Hitchcock, and Barbara Hull. His work has appeared in various periodicals over the last thirty-five years, as well as the anthologies *Good Poems, American Places*, *Hunger Enough*, *Retail Woes*, and *Line Drives*. He has also been nominated for both Pushcart Prizes and The Best of the Net. Two full-length collections are in the works: *Lent 1999* is coming soon from Leaf Garden Press and *This Twilight World* will be published by Popcorn Press. His chapbook, *Three Visitors* has recently been published by Negative Capability Press. *Artifacts and Relics*, another chapbook, is forthcoming from Folded Word, and his novel, *Knight Prisoner*, was recently published by Vagabondage Press and a another novel, *A Book of Lost Songs* is coming soon from Wild Child Publishing. He lives in San Francisco with his wife, the documentarian and filmmaker, Joan Juster.

ALLEN FORREST is a graphic artist and painter born in Canada and bred in the U.S. He has created cover art and illustrations for literary publications and books. He is the winner of the Leslie Jacoby Honor for Art at San Jose State University's Reed Magazine and his Bel Red painting series is part of the

Bellevue College Foundation's permanent art collection. Forrest's expressive drawing and painting style is a mix of avant-garde expressionism and post-Impressionist elements reminiscent of van Gogh, creating emotion on canvas.

CONNOR WOOD is a writer and conservation biologist. He is leaving New England after nine years for Madison, Wisconsin. This is his first published fiction; his non-fiction has appeared in the *New Mexico Review*. Connect via @connormmw

LIZ PURVIS is an MFA candidate in poetry at NC State, poetry editor for *The Fem*, and recipient of the E. Nelson James Award for "What I Mean to Say But Haven't," a poem published in The *Sigma Tau Delta Rectangle*. Her publications include pieces in *Cahoodaloodaling*, *Damselfly Press*, *Deep South Magazine*, and others.

TOM LARSEN has been a fiction writer for fifteen years and his work has appeared in *Newsday*, *Best American Mystery Stories*, *Puerto del Sol* and the *LA Review*. His novels *Flawed* and *Into the Fire* are available through Crime Wave Press.

Maybe we will see each other again.